Grand
Are Fun!

by Margie Sigman

HOUGHTON MIFFLIN BOSTON

There are many kinds of grandparents.

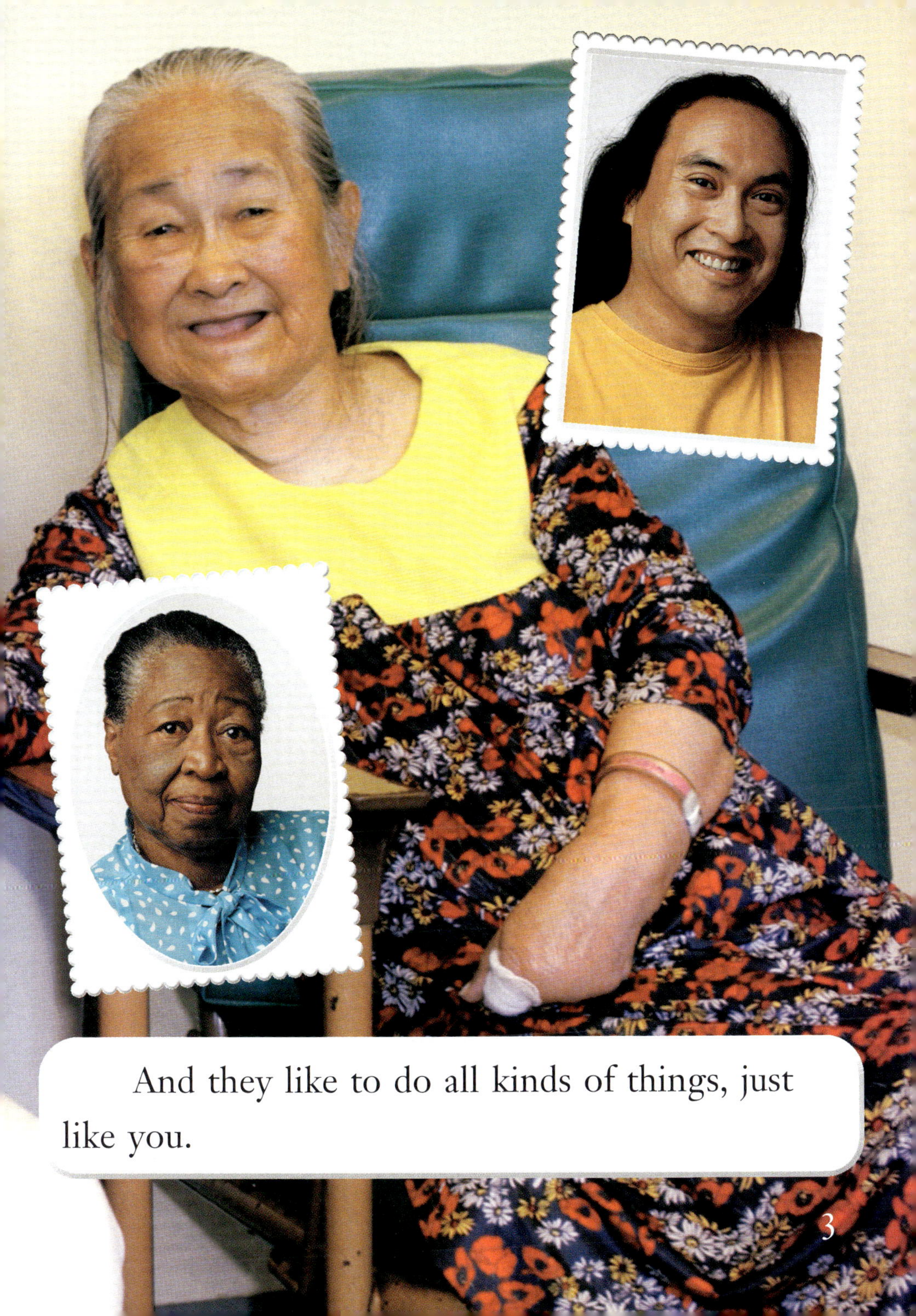

And they like to do all kinds of things, just like you.

Some grandparents like to ride bikes. Some like to play games.

Some grandparents like to go to movies. Some like to eat pizza.

Ana has two grandfathers and two grandmothers. She sees them almost every day. One grandmother picks her up at school. One grandfather comes to all her soccer games.

Sofia and Tony are twins. They live with their grandfather, Mr. Lopez, and his mother. She is Sofia's and Tony's great-grandmother.

Mr. Jackson has ten grandchildren and two great-grandchildren. He likes to send them e-mails. He writes them letters, jokes, and photos.

Many grandparents work. Some work in offices. Others work in stores. Darrell loves to visit his grandmother at her job. She teaches children how to ride horses.

Some grandparents don't work any more. They can spend more time with their families. Michael and his grandfather like to fish together.

Mark's grandmother works at his school. She is a volunteer. She does not get paid to work. She reads books to children and listens to them read to her.

Grandparents are older than you. But they still know how to have fun. That's why grandparents make great friends!